Changing Shape

Paul Bennett

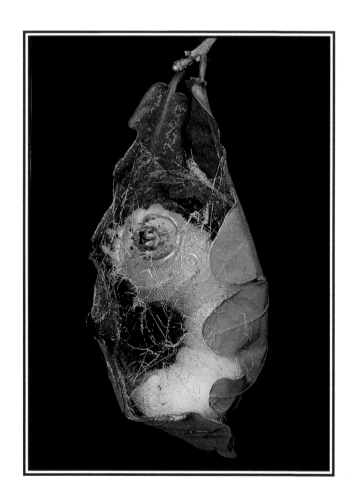

Wayland

Nature's Secrets

Cover : Common frog and tadpoles.
Title page: Silk moth cocoon.
Contents page: Dragonfly nymph.

Series editor: Francesca Motisi
Book editor: Francesca Motisi
Designer: Joyce Chester
Consultant: Stephen Savage

First published in 1994 by
Wayland (Publishers) Ltd
61 Western Road, Hove
East Sussex BN3 1JD, England

© Copyright 1994 Wayland (Publishers) Ltd

British Library Cataloguing in Publication Data

Bennett, Paul
  Changing Shape. (Nature's Secrets Series)
  I. Title II. Series
  591.3

ISBN 0-7502-1062-1

Printed and bound in Italy by
G. Canale & C.S.p.A., Turin

Picture acknowledgements
The publishers would like to thank the following for allowing their photographs to be reproduced in this book: Bruce Coleman Ltd cover (main/P. Clement, inset/Kim Taylor), 18 (above/Jane Burton, below/Udo Hirsch), 19 (Jane Burton), 20 (below/Jane Burton), 23 (below/George McCarthy), 24 (Jane Burton), 25 (below/Michael Glover), 29 (above and middle/Kim Taylor); the Natural History Photographic Agency 6, 7, 8, 9, 10, 11, 14 (all Stephen Dalton), 15 (above/Stephen Dalton, below John Shaw), 16, 17, 20 above, 21, 22, 23 above (Stephen Dalton); Oxford Scientific Films Ltd 5 (above/George K. Bryce, below/K. G. Voak), 12 (above/Avril Ramage, below/Harold Taylor), 13 (Neil Bromhall), 26 (G. I. Bernard), 27 (above/Harold Taylor, below/Fredrik Ehrenstrom), 28 (J. A. L. Cooke), 29 (bottom/Rudie H. Kuiter); Planet Earth Pictures 25 (above/Robert Arnold); Wayland Picture Library 4 (both).

Contents

Introduction

Have you ever been given a kitten as a pet? Or maybe a young rat, hamster or goldfish? All these baby creatures look just like their parents. But there are many baby animals that must change their shape before they become adults. This change that takes place is called metamorphosis.

△ There are many baby creatures that look like small versions of their parents. Kittens are cuddly and they look just like small cats.

◁ Babies look like small versions of you or me.

△ Maggots are
not at all like
adult flies. They
must change their
shape and go
through
metamorphosis
before they
become like their
parents. ▷

Butterflies

There are thousands of types of insects and nearly all of them must change their shape before they become adults. Butterflies go through dramatic changes during their lives. Before they are fully grown they must pass through the stages of egg, larva (caterpillar), pupa (chrysalis) and adult.

◁ Most butterfly eggs are laid on a plant that the young caterpillar will eat. Out of an egg will hatch a caterpillar or larva. It may be smooth or hairy, or may have long spines, depending on the type of butterfly. The tiny eggs of the swallowtail butterfly are stuck to the underside of a leaf. Larvae (caterpillars) hatch out of the eggs.

◁ The caterpillars have many legs and biting jaws. As they grow, they shed their skins many times.

After it has shed its skin several times, the larva stops feeding and changes into a pupa or chrysalis. Inside its hard case, the whole body changes, while the wings, legs and body of the adult insect develop. ▷

△ Inside its ugly pupa the caterpillar
changes into a beautiful butterfly. The
butterfly emerges by splitting open the
case. Its wings are crumpled at first
and have to be pumped up with blood
to make them open up.

After about an hour, the butterfly
begins to look like a real adult.
It is ready to fly away. ▽

Moths

△ This fat, green grub is a silk moth larva. Like the butterfly larva, it eats leaves all day long.

◁ Now it is spinning a snug cocoon, a soft covering of silk to protect it while it changes into a pupa.

Then, like the butterfly larva, it changes
from a pupa into a fully grown moth.

Ladybirds

The ladybird lays her tiny eggs on a leaf. Soon they hatch and strange-looking larvae emerge.

Ladybird larvae eat lots of juicy greenfly. As they grow they become too big for their skins. They moult their skins several times. ▽

When the larva has eaten enough food,
it changes into a pupa. Inside, a
ladybird beetle is ready to come out.

△ The young beetle is yellow and its
spots are very faint. Soon its wings will
dry and it will fly away. In a few days,
it will have its familiar bright red
colouring and black spots.

Honey-bees

Looking like a space-man, the bee-keeper releases a new queen honey-bee into the hive. The bee-keeper's clothes prevent him from being stung. ▷

The queen bee has laid these delicate eggs in the cells of the hive. ▽

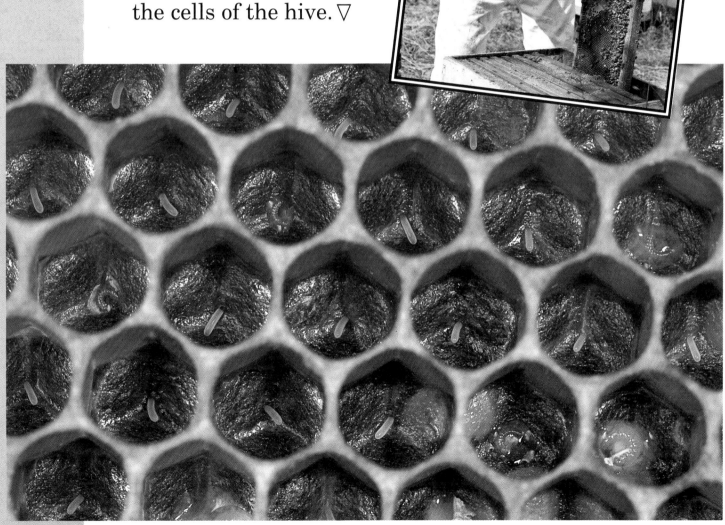

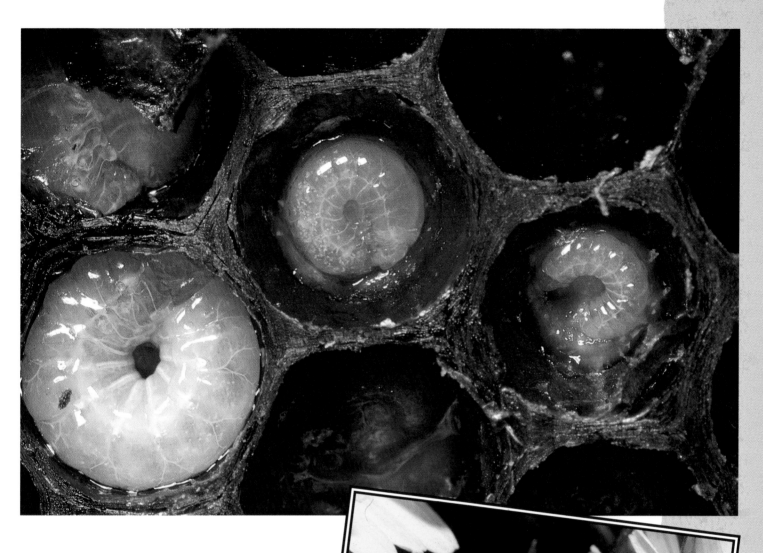

△ The eggs hatch and grow. The grubs curl themselves into a C-shape at the bottom of the cell.

A worker bee gathers pollen on its hind legs. ▷

◁ Worker bees feed the growing grubs on pollen and honey.

△ The larvae have changed into white pupae. Now they are beginning to look like adult bees.

An adult bee hatches from its cell. Soon it will be busy collecting pollen and nectar from flowers. ▷

Dragonflies

Dragonflies change gradually in stages - there is no pupal stage. At each stage, the nymphs look more and more like adults. A dragonfly lays its eggs carefully in a pond. The nymphs will emerge to spend up to three years underwater.

The nymph hunts for food. As it grows, its wing 'buds' develop and it moults its skin. ▷

The fully grown nymph leaves the water. It crawls up a plant and digs its claws into the stem.

◁ The old skin of the nymph splits open to let the adult emerge.

△ It takes a few days for the bright colours of the dragonfly to develop fully. Then it can be seen near water, darting after insects which are its food.

Frogs and toads

Frogs and toads nearly always lay
their eggs in water and that is where
they grow bigger. The eggs of frogs
look like little black dots in a mass
of jelly. ▽

Toads' eggs are laid
in ribbons which
wrap around water
plants. ▷

When the eggs hatch, thousands of wriggling tadpoles come out from the eggs or spawn. They have tiny round heads and tails. Only a few will live long enough to become adult frogs because other pond creatures like to eat them. ▽

A young tadpole has no legs. It breathes oxygen through tiny gills on the side of its head and it lives in the water like a fish. It eats algae and pondweed.

△ As the tadpole feeds, it starts to grow. Back legs appear and it develops lungs for breathing air.

Soon the tadpole ▷ has front legs. As its body grows, its tail becomes smaller and smaller. It begins to look like a frog.

The baby frog or froglet is soon strong enough to hop out of the water on to the land. Its webbed feet are good for swimming. ▷

At last, the ▷ froglet's tail is gone and it becomes a tiny frog, just like its mother only much smaller.

While the baby frog is growing into an adult frog it lives near the water. Frogs are amphibious, which means that they can live on land and in water.

Lobsters

△ Many lobsters and crabs live on the sea-bed. They have hard shells which cannot stretch and when they grow they must shed their shells, like this Pacific lobster.

The female lobster carries around thousands of eggs until they are ready to hatch. When the eggs are ready to hatch, she releases her babies into the sea. A baby lobster does not look a bit like its mother. It is transparent and drifts near the surface of the sea. As it grows it moults its tiny shell. After several moults it changes into a larva and looks more like a lobster. This is the larva of the squat lobster. ▷

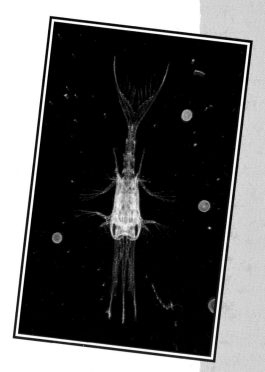

△ As it grows it continues to shed its shell and settles on the sea-bed. Underneath is a new, soft shell which hardens in about three days. This is a fully grown squat lobster feeding.

Crabs

The female crab carries her eggs tucked under her tail. ▽

This female spider crab releases her tiny larvae. As she lets them go, the larvae form a dark-looking cloud in the water. ▷

Before they settle on the sea-bed, the tiny crab and lobster larvae can be carried for thousands of kilometres from the place they were born. They are part of a drifting community of creatures called plankton. ▷

Fish

Some fish that live on the sea-bed
change their shape. Adult plaice and
sole like to lie buried in the sand where
they are protected from their enemies.
Their bodies are flat with their eyes on
top, but they were not born like that.
They were born with an eye on each
side of their head.

A larva that hatches from the ▷
eggs is tiny - about 5 mm long.
It has a normal fish shape and
swims near the surface of the sea.
Then after about twenty days one
eye moves so that both eyes are
on the same side of its body.

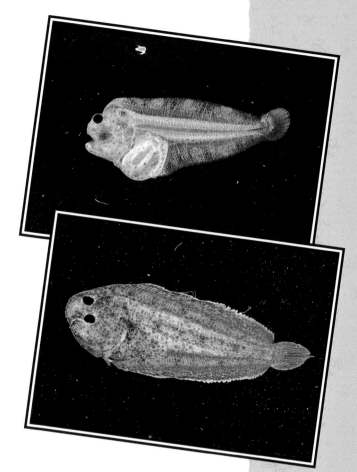

After about two months the larva
gradually changes into a flat fish.
It starts swimming more on its
side and its head grows more
quickly on one side than the
other. ▷

△ After completing its metamorphosis
the sole now settles on the sea-bed
where it spends the rest of its life. Its
eyes and mouth are slightly crooked.

Glossary

Caterpillar The larva of an insect that feeds on leaves.

Cells The small compartments or 'rooms' that make up the nests of bees and wasps.

Chrysalis The pupa of a moth or butterfly in a case.

Cocoon The covering or case spun by a larva to protect it while it turns into an adult.

Dramatic Unexpected or sudden.

Gills The parts of a tadpole's body that enable it to breathe.

Grub Another word for larva.

Hive A place made by people for bees to live in and produce honey.

Larva An insect in its first stage after coming out of the egg.

Moulting Shedding a skin.

Nymphs Insects not yet fully developed.

Pupa The stage when an insect changes from a larva to an adult.

Queen honey-bee The only properly developed female honey-bee in a hive.

Shed To throw or cast off.

Transparent Able to be seen through.

Books to read

Discovering Nature series (Wayland): A series of books that takes a wide look at animals and plants. It includes titles on ants, bees and wasps, beetles, butterflies and moths, crabs and lobsters, crickets and grasshoppers, damselflies and dragonflies, flies, frogs.

Life cycles series (Wayland): The books in this series provide an explanation of each stage in a creature's life. Look for titles on ants, bees, butterflies, crabs, frogs, grasshoppers, ladybirds and toads.

Notes for parents and teachers

Examples of metamorphoses can be observed in an old aquarium tank.

Project: **Butterfly Life Cycle**

Materials: Small aquarium tank with fine mesh lid.

In the late spring/early summer, collect butterfly eggs that have been laid on plants. Decorate the tank with twigs etc. Place the eggs in the tank and wait for them to hatch. You will need to collect a constant supply of food for the hungry caterpillars. You must feed them on the same type of plant that the eggs were found on, eg. the caterpillars of the peacock butterfly and the small tortoise shell butterfly feed on stinging nettles.

You can observe each caterpillar shed its skin as it grows and changes into a chrysalis. Eventually, the adult butterflies will hatch out. You should then release the butterflies in the areas where you collected the eggs.

You can attract butterflies to your garden by planting buddleia, ice plant, or many other flowering plants that butterflies feed on. If you want them to lay eggs, you will have to provide the right food-plants.

Project: **Frog Life Cycle**

Materials: Aquarium tank with tight-fitting lid.

Cover the bottom of the aquarium with gravel and half fill with water. Pond or rain water is best. If using tap water, allow it to stand for forty-eight hours to allow the chlorine to escape. Use some rocks, slate and bog wood to create a small area that is just above water level. Use plenty of pond plants such as Canadian pondweed and hornwort.

Collect frogspawn in the spring and watch the eggs develop. It is best to collect them from a garden pond if you can. When they hatch, they will feed on algae in the water and on the plants. As they get bigger, you can feed the tadpoles on a small amount of fish food. Watch them develop into small frogs. The baby frogs will start to climb on to the raised area. It is important to have a raised area, because the baby frogs are very vulnerable to drowning at this stage.

Return the young frogs to the pond where you collected the spawn. Do not try to raise these young frogs yourself, because it is very difficult to provide enough tiny creatures as food.

You can attract frogs and other amphibians to your garden by providing a pond. Not only will this help conserve the frogs but as a bonus they will also feed on slugs and your other garden pests.

Places to visit: Some of the unusual animals discussed in this book may be seen if you visit a Public Aquarium, Wildlife Trust Reserve or a Butterfly Farm.

Index